30 DAY WHOLE FOOD CHALLENGE

30 Day Whole Food Challenge

Whole Food Cookbook with 30 Day Meal Plan; Approved Whole Food Recipes for Rapid Weight Loss and Optimal Health

Christos Sarantos

Contents

Whole Food Dinner Recipes

What is the Whole Food Diet?

The Whole Food Diet is based on the philosophy that eating healthy means eating fresh, natural foods that are unprocessed and free of chemical additives. This radically simple approach to what we consume has started a revolution, with people all around the globe making the decision to "fight back" against the onslaught of processed "Franken-foods" that fill our grocery store shelves and are served in paper bags from drive-thru windows. Taking control of the food you eat begins with a simple 30 day challenge. Stick to the rules for 3 meals a day for 30 days and see how you feel. *Chances are you will be a whole food convert for life.*

Foods You CAN Consume on The Whole Food Diet.

You can enjoy all of the following foods without breaking any rules:

> **MEAT:** You can have chicken, pork, beef, turkey, deli meat and other meats. However, you CAN NOT have meats that are processed with added sugar, MSG, sulfites or carrageenan.
> **EGGS**
> **SEAFOOD:** Salmon, prawns, white fish, scallops and other seafood are all available for you to enjoy, once again avoid any seafood that is processed.
> **VEGETABLES:** All types of vegetables are available on the Whole Food Diet.
> **FRUIT:** All kinds of fruits are acceptable on the Whole Food Diet.
> **COOKING FATS:** You can include clarified butter, ghee, duck fat, lard, tallow, palm oil, coconut oil, and extra-virgin olive oil.
> **NUTS AND SEEDS:** Eat nuts and seeds only in moderation.
> **DRESSINGS:** Avocado, avocado oil, shredded coconut, coconut flakes, coconut butter, canned coconut, olives, sesame oil, and light olive oil are all acceptable dressings on the Whole Food Diet.
> **HERBS AND SPICES:** When you are using commercially packaged herbs and spices always check the labels to see if they have anything that is against the rules.
> **DRINKS:** Club soda, coconut water, vegetable juice, fruit juice, sparkling water, apple cider, coffee, mineral water, naturally flavored water, seltzer water, tea, 100% cacao drink and kombucha are all acceptable.

Foods to AVOID when on the Whole Food Diet

The following foods should be avoided while following the Whole Food Diet:

> Added sugar
> Grains
> Alcohol — as a drink and as additions in food.
> Legumes — all kinds of beans, lentils, chickpeas, peas. Except for those listed above.
> All soy — soy sauce, tofu, tempeh, miso, edamame.
> Dairy
> MSG, sulfites and carrageen.
> Vinegar with added sugar and malt vinegar.

CHAPTER 1

Whole Food Breakfast Recipes

Carrot & Mixed Fruit Smoothie

Ingredients

½ pineapple (peeled)

1 orange (peeled)

1 banana (peeled)

1 apple

1 cup strawberries (frozen)

1 cup grapes (seedless)

3 baby carrots

Instructions:

- Combine all the ingredients in a blender and blend well.

- Chill.

Makes: 6 servings

Nutritional information per serving:

Calories: 159.8; Total Fat: 0.7 g; Carbohydrates: 41.3 g; Proteins: 1.2 g

Breakfast Bowl

Ingredients

1 banana (mashed)

2 eggs

½ apple (chopped)

1 tablespoon almond butter

1 tablespoon coconut flakes

Pinch of ground cinnamon

Instructions:

- Combine together the mashed banana and eggs and whisk together.

- Cook the mixture in a pan just as you cook scrambled eggs.

- Transfer the cooked mixture into a bowl and mix in the almond butter.

- Add the apples and coconut flakes.

- Sprinkle a pinch of cinnamon.

Makes: 1 serving

Nutritional information per serving:

Calories: 395 kcal; Total Fat: 18.39 g; Carbohydrates: 45.95 g; Proteins: 16.79 g

Basil Zucchini Omelette

Ingredients

½ teaspoon olive oil

½ cup zucchini (diced)

½ cup tomatoes (diced)

2 tablespoons basil

2 eggs

1 egg white

Salt and pepper to taste

Instructions:

- Heat oil in a skillet and sauté the tomatoes and zucchini in it, seasoning it with salt and pepper. Mix in the basil and place aside.

- Whisk together the egg white and eggs with some salt and pepper and pour into the pan greased with cooking spray.

- Cook on both sides until done.

- Transfer the egg onto a platter, scoop the sautéed veggies at the centre and then fold the egg over.

Makes: 1 serving

Nutritional information per serving:

Calories: 205; Total Fat: 12 g; Carbohydrates: 6 g; Proteins: 19 g

Butternut Sausage Breakfast Casserole

Ingredients

1 lb lean turkey sausage (ground)

2 teaspoons olive oil

2 cups butternut squash (peeled, diced)

½ red onion (diced)

½ teaspoon salt

½ teaspoon garlic powder

½ teaspoon pepper

½ teaspoon oregano

4 egg whites

4 cups spinach (chopped)

4 eggs

Instructions:

- Heat a skillet and cook the sausage in it, breaking it up until no longer pink. Place aside.

- Heat the olive oil in the skillet and sauté the onion and squash in it for 8-10 minutes, adding tablespoons of water to prevent burning.

- Season with the spices and add the spinach, cooking until wilted.

- Transfer the mixture in a baking dish greased with cooking spray.

- Whisk together the egg and egg whites and pour it over the veggie mixture.

- Bake in an oven preheated to 400 degrees Fahrenheit for 25-30 minutes till the eggs are cooked and set.

Makes: 4 servings

Nutritional information per serving:

Calories: 331; Total Fat: 16 g; Carbohydrates: 12 g; Proteins: 33 g

Sausage & Sweet Potato Scramble

Ingredients

½ cup sweet potatoes (diced, cooked)

½ cup breakfast sausage (cooked)

2 eggs (scrambled)

1 teaspoon coconut oil

Salt and Pepper to taste

Garlic powder to taste

Paprika to taste

Instructions:

- Heat the oil in a skillet and sauté the sausage and sweet potatoes in it until lightly heated.

- Add the eggs to the skillet and mix well, cooking until the egg is no longer runny.

- Mix in the rest of the ingredients.

Makes: 1 serving

Nutritional information per serving:

Calories: 366; Total Fat: 24 g; Carbohydrates: 19 g; Proteins: 19 g

Almond Flavoured Banana & Coconut flakes

Ingredients

1 banana (sliced)

2 tablespoon almond butter

1 tablespoon coconut flakes

Instructions:

- Toss together the banana slices and the almond butter.

- Sprinkle the coconut flakes on top.

Makes: 1 serving

Nutritional information per serving:

Calories: 105; Total Fat: 0 g; Carbohydrates: 27 g; Proteins: 1 g

Berries & Nuts in Coconut Milk

Ingredients

½ cup berries (seasonal)

¼ cup almonds

1 can coconut milk

Instructions:

- Combine all the ingredients and stir well.

Makes: 2 servings

Nutritional information per serving:

Calories: 493; Total Fat: 50 g; Carbohydrates: 12 g; Proteins: 8 g

Vegetable & Avocado Scramble

Ingredients

2 teaspoon olive oil

2 cups broccoli (chopped)

1 red pepper (chopped)

½ cup onion (diced)

8 eggs (whisked)

1 tomato (diced)

1 avocado (chopped)

Salt and pepper to taste

Instructions:

- Heat olive oil in a pan and sauté the onion, broccoli, red pepper in it for 3-4 minutes until crispy tender.

- Mix in the eggs, stirring often until done.

- Mix in the tomato and avocado and season with salt and pepper.

Makes: 4 servings

Nutritional information per serving:

Calories: 279; Total Fat: 19 g; Carbohydrates: 12 g; Proteins: 16 g

Butter Sausage & Apple Hash

Ingredients

1 ½ lean turkey sausage (ground)

2 teaspoon olive oil

½ sweet onion (diced)

1 red pepper (chopped)

6 cups butternut squash (peeled, chopped)

1 apple (chopped)

2 garlic cloves (minced)

½ teaspoon dried rosemary

Salt and pepper to taste

Instructions:

- Heat a skillet greased with cooking spray and brown the sausage in it for 4-5 minutes. Place aside.

- Heat the olive oil and sauté the red pepper, onion, squash and apple in it for 8-10 minutes until the squash is tender, adding tablespoons of water to avoid burning.

- Mix in the rosemary and garlic, cooking for a minute.

- Season with salt and pepper and mix the cooked sausage back in.

Makes: 6 servings

Nutritional information per serving:

Calories: 285; Total Fat: 11 g; Carbohydrates: 25 g; Proteins: 23 g

Spinach & Sweet Potato Breakfast Casserole

Ingredients

2 teaspoon olive oil

3 cups sweet potato (peeled, diced)

½ red onion (diced)

½ teaspoon salt

½ teaspoon garlic powder

½ teaspoon oregano

½ teaspoon pepper

4 cups spinach (chopped)

8 eggs

Instructions:

- Heat olive oil in a pan and cook the onion and sweet potatoes in it for 8-10 minutes, adding tablespoons of water to prevent burning.

- Season with the spices and add the spinach, cooking until wilted.

- Transfer the mixture in a baking dish greased with cooking spray.

- Whisk together the eggs and pour it over the veggie mixture.

- Bake in an oven preheated to 400 degrees Fahrenheit for 25-30 minutes till the eggs are cooked and set.

Makes: 4 servings

Nutritional information per serving:

Calories: 264; Total Fat: 12 g; Carbohydrates: 24 g; Proteins: 15 g

Breakfast Veggie Frittata

Ingredients

½ onion (sliced)

1 cup cauliflower (chopped)

1 carrot (julienned)

½ red bell pepper

2 kale leaves (chopped finely)

2 tomatoes (sliced)

5 eggs

Cracked bell pepper to taste

Oil for frying

Instructions:

- Heat some oil in a skillet and cook the carrots, cauliflower and onion in it until lightly browned and tender, adding water if required.

- Add the kale and bell pepper, reduce the flame and cook for 3-5 minutes, stirring often.

- Beat the eggs in a bowl and add some black pepper to it.

- Spread the mixture in the skillet and arrange the tomato slices on top.

- Pour the egg over and cook for 3-5 minutes.

- Place the pan under a preheated broiler and cook until the top is golden brown.

Makes: 2 servings

Nutritional information per serving:

Calories: 271; Total Fat: 12.6 g; Carbohydrates: 13.7 g; Proteins: 20.2 g

Breakfast Green Smoothie

Ingredients

½ avocado (peeled, chopped, pit discarded)

Handful of spinach

Handful of kale

1¼ cup coconut water

1 small cucumber (chopped)

1¾ oz pineapple chunks

Instructions:

- Combine all the ingredients in a high speed blender.

- Blend until smooth.

Makes: 1 serving

Nutritional information per serving:

Calories: 262 kcal; Total Fat: 16 g; Carbohydrates: 21 g; Proteins: 8 g

Sweet Potato & Chicken Sausage Hash

Ingredients

4 tablespoon olive oil

1 sweet potato (diced)

3 oz yellow bell pepper (diced)

3 oz red bell pepper (diced)

2 garlic cloves (minced)

1lb chicken sausage (ground)

5 oz onion (diced)

1 green onion (chopped)

Sea salt and black pepper to taste

Instructions:

- Heat half the oil in a pan and sauté the sweet potatoes, garlic and peppers in it until lightly browned.

- In another skillet, heat the rest of the oil and sauté the onions, chicken sausage, salt and pepper in it until the sausage is no longer pink.

- Mix together the ingredients of both pans and serve garnished with the green onions.

Makes: 6 servings

Nutritional information per serving:

Calories: 214; Total Fat: 13.5 g; Carbohydrates: 8 g; Proteins: 11.5 g

Sweet Potato & Sausage Breakfast Bake

Ingredients

½ tablespoon coconut oil

1 sweet potato (cubed)

½ lb turkey sausage

½ red onion (sliced)

½ red bell pepper (sliced)

7 eggs

3 cups spinach

Sea salt and Pepper to taste

1 Avocado (sliced)

Instructions:

- Heat coconut oil in a pan and add the sweet potato to it with a dash of salt, cooking covered for 10 minutes, stirring occasionally.

- Heat another pan and brown the sausage in it for 4-5 minutes.

- Add the onion and bell pepper and cook for 2-3 minutes after which add the spinach and leave to wilt for 2 minutes.

- Whisk the eggs together with salt and pepper.

- Grease a glass dish with coconut spray and layer the sweet potatoes in it. Layer the turkey sausage next and then layer the veggies mixture. Finally spread the whisked eggs.

- Bake for 16-18 minutes in an oven preheated to 400 degrees Fahrenheit.

- Remove and leave aside for 5 minutes, topping with avocado slices.

Makes: 4 servings

Nutritional information per serving:

Calories: 330; Total Fat: 18 g; Carbohydrates: 16 g; Proteins: 24 g

Coconut & Orange Omelette

Ingredients

3 eggs

¼ cup full-fat coconut milk

½ teaspoon orange zest

1 tablespoon coconut oil

Salt and pepper to taste

Instructions:

- Heat the oil in a non-stick pan.

- Combine the rest of the ingredients in a bowl and whisk till frothy.

- Pour the egg mixture into the pan and spread it.

- Leave to cook and then flip to cook on the other side.

- Transfer onto a platter.

Makes: 1 serving

Nutritional information per serving:

Calories: 433; Total Fat: 38.5 g; Carbohydrates: 3 g; Proteins: 19.9 g

Pork & Blackberry Breakfast Sausage

Ingredients

1 lb pork (ground)

½ teaspoon ground sage (dried)

½ teaspoon dried thyme

½ teaspoon garlic powder

1 teaspoon sea salt

½ cup fresh blackberries (chopped)

Pinch of black pepper

Coconut oil to fry

Instructions:

- Combine all the ingredients except the oil and blackberries in a bowl and mix well.

- Mix in the blackberries and then shape portions of the mixture into 8 patties.

- Heat some coconut oil in a skillet and place the patties in it in batches cooking for 2-3 minutes per side.

- Transfer onto a platter.

Makes: 8 servings

Nutritional information per serving:

Calories: 110; Total fat: 12 g; Carbohydrates: 1 g; Proteins: 10 g

Whole Food Approved Bacon & Root Veggie Hash

Ingredients

6 thick-cut Whole Food Approved bacon slices (with

no added sugar)

8 oz sweet potato (diced)

8 oz beets (peeled, diced)

8 oz white turnip (diced)

3 oz red onion

3 garlic cloves (minced)

1 celery rib (diced)

Sea salt and pepper to taste

Instructions:

- Cook the bacon slices in a pan until crispy and place aside.

- Add the rest of the ingredients to the bacon fat in the pan and stir cook for 15-20 minutes until the veggies become tender.

- Crumble the bacon and add it back to the pan.

Makes: 6 servings

Nutritional information per serving:

Calories: 105; Total Fat: 4 g; Carbohydrates: 11 g; Proteins: 4 g

Double-Baked Breakfast Potatoes

Ingredients

2 sweet potatoes

4 Whole Food Approved bacon pieces (no sugar added)

1 onion

4 garlic cloves (minced)

4 eggs

Salt and pepper to taste

Instructions:

- Using a fork poke the potatoes and then place them on an oven rack.

- Cook in an oven preheated to 400 degrees Fahrenheit for 40-45 minutes. Leave aside to cool.

- Chop the potatoes lengthwise and scoop the centre out.

- Cook the bacon in a skillet until crispy and transfer into a bowl. Dice after it is cooled.

- Sauté the onion and garlic in the bacon fat.

- Mash the scooped portion of the sweet potato in the skillet, cooking covered for 10 minutes.

- Season with salt and pepper and mix in the bacon pieces.

- Scoop the mixture into the shells of the potato and make some space for an egg.

- Break an egg into each half and place the stuffed potatoes on a parchment lined baking sheet.

- Bake for 15 minutes until the egg sets.

Makes: 4 servings

Nutritional information per serving:

Calories: 1526; Total Fat: 152 g; Carbohydrates: 20 g; Proteins: 76 g

Breakfast Pork Sausages

Ingredients

12 oz pork (ground)

1 teaspoon fennel seeds

½ teaspoon crushed red pepper

1 teaspoon oregano

Salt and pepper to taste

Instructions:

- Combine all the ingredients in a bowl and mix well.

- Shape portions of the mixture into patties.

- Cook covered in a skillet over medium flame for around 3 minutes per side.

Makes: 6 servings

Nutritional information per serving:

Calories: 171; Total Fat: 12 g; Carbohydrates: 0 g; Proteins: 15 g

Breakfast Chia Pudding

Ingredients

12 cashews

3 cups water

3 tablespoon hemp seeds

3 small dates

½ teaspoon cinnamon

6 tablespoons chia seeds

Pinch of sea salt

Instructions:

- Combine the hemp seeds, dates, cashews and a cup of water in a blender, blending until smooth.

- Add in the rest of the ingredients and pulse until mixed.

- Refrigerate for 2-3 hours.

Makes: 3 servings

Nutritional information per serving:

Calories: 236; Total Fat: 15 g; Carbohydrates: 21 g; Proteins: 8 g

Chorizo & Kale Hash with Sweet Potatoes

Ingredients

8 oz raw chorizo (casings removed)

1 tablespoon olive oil

2 cups sweet potato (chopped)

½ cup onion (chopped)

2 cups kale (chopped)

1 teaspoon garlic powder

1 teaspoon cumin

1 tablespoon lime juice

Salt and pepper to taste

Instructions:

- Sauté the chorizo in a pan for 4-5 minutes and place aside.

- Add the sweet potatoes, olive oil, cumin and garlic powder to the same pan and stir cook for 5 minutes.

- Add the chorizo back to the pan along with the onions and cook for 5 minutes more.

- Mix in the kale, cooking for 2 minutes until wilted.

- Remove from the flame and mix in the rest of the ingredients.

Makes: 4 servings

Nutritional information per serving:

Calories: 255; Total Fat: 17 g; Carbohydrates: 16 g; Proteins: 9 g

Breakfast Ham & Potato Frittata

Ingredients

1 tablespoon olive oil

1 onion (chopped)

2 baking potato (peeled, sliced thinly)

1 cup ham (diced)

1 tomato (sliced thinly)

6 organic eggs

¼ cup fresh chives (chopped)

Salt and pepper to taste

Instructions:

- Heat oil in a skillet and cook the potatoes in it for 10 minutes covered, stirring occasionally.

- Add the onions and cook for another 2 minutes.

- Sprinkle the ham on top.

- Whisk together the eggs, salt, pepper and chives in a bowl and then pour it into the skillet.

- Place the tomato slices on top and cook covered for a minute.

- Place the skillet beneath a preheated broiler, 3 inches from the heat and cook until the eggs set for around 3 minutes.

Makes: 8 servings

Nutritional information per serving:

Calories: 136; Total Fat: 7 g; Carbohydrates: 10.3 g; Proteins: 8.7 g

Summer Veggie-Egg Breakfast

Ingredients

1 tablespoon olive oil

2 courgettes (chopped)

7 oz cherry tomatoes (halved)

1 garlic clove (crushed)

2 eggs

Basil leaves for garnish

Salt and pepper

Instructions:

- Heat oil in a pan and sauté the courgettes in it for 5 minutes, stirring often.

- Add the garlic and tomatoes and cook for another couple of minutes.

- Season with salt and pepper and make two gaps for the eggs.

- Crack the eggs into the two gaps and cook covered for 2-3 minutes.

- Serve garnished with basil leaves.

Makes: 2 servings

Nutritional information per serving:

Calories: 196kcal; Total Fat: 13 g; Carbohydrates: 7 g; Proteins: 12 g

Asian Seafood Omelette

Ingredients

4 eggs (beaten)

½ lemon (juiced)

Handful of small broccoli florets

1 red chilli (chopped)

1 garlic clove (chopped)

7 oz prawns (cooked)

Sunflower oil for cooking

Instructions:

- Heat oil in a pan and sauté the broccoli in it for 2 minutes.

- Add the garlic, chilli and prawns and leave to cook until the broccoli is done.

- Transfer the mixture onto a platter.

- Beat together the eggs and lemon juice and pour half the mixture onto the pan swirling it around.

- Flip and cook on the other side. Transfer onto a platter.

- Repeat with the remaining egg.

- Distribute the prawn mixture between the 2 omelettes and roll up.

Makes: 2 servings

Nutritional information per serving:

Calories: 386kcal; Total Fat: 25 g; Carbohydrates: 1 g; Proteins: 39 g

Scotch Eggs

Ingredients

6 boiled eggs (peeled)

1 lb pork (minced)

½ teaspoon salt

2 teaspoon parsley

Instructions:

- Combine the pork, parsley and salt in a bowl and mix well.

- Flatten a portion of pork mixture on your hand, place the egg on it and gradually cover the egg with the pork mince.

- Repeat with all eggs and then arrange them on an oiled baking tray.

- Cook in an oven preheated to 350 degrees Fahrenheit for 30 minutes.

Makes: 6 servings

Nutritional information per serving:

Calories: 167; Total Fat: 9.8 g; Carbohydrates: 0 g; Proteins: 20.7 g

Mexicana Breakfast Bowl

Ingredients

5 ¼ oz grass-fed ground beef

½ teaspoon cumin

¼ teaspoon ground chipotle

¼ teaspoon onion powder

1 tomato (diced)

2 boiled eggs (peeled, mashed)

¼ yellow bell pepper (diced)

½ ripe avocado (diced)

10 black olives (pitted, chopped into half)

1 teaspoon extra-virgin olive oil

1 teaspoon white wine vinegar

1 tablespoon Whole30 friendly mayo

½ lime (juiced)

Salt and pepper to taste

Fresh coriander leaves (for garnish)

Instructions:

- Marinate the avocado with salt, pepper, vinegar and oil.

- Heat a skillet and add the beef, cumin, chipotle, onion powder and half the tomato, cooking for a minute, stirring occasionally.

- Transfer the mixture into a bowl and spread it.

- Layer the eggs over it, then the bell peppers and finally the rest of the tomatoes.

- Sprinkle the black olives on top followed by the avocado.

- Add the mayo on top, sprinkle the lime juice and garnish with coriander.

Makes: 1 serving

Nutritional information per serving:

Calories: 588; Total Fat: 36.7 g; Carbohydrates: 21.4 g; Proteins: 48.3 g

Baked Mushroom Omelette

Ingredients

4 eggs

1 cup mushrooms (cubed)

1 cup frozen spinach (thawed, drained)

½ cup onions (chopped)

1 tablespoon extra-light olive oil

Instructions:

- Heat oil in a skillet and sauté the onions and mushrooms in it.

- Add the spinach and cook for a couple of minutes.

- Leave to cool and then mix in the eggs, transferring the mixture into a greased baking dish.

- Bake in an oven preheated to 350 degrees Fahrenheit for 10-15 minutes.

Makes: 4 servings

Nutritional information per serving:

Calories: 123.8; Total Fat: 8.5 g; Carbohydrates: 4.4 g; Proteins: 8.4 g

Egg & Beef Breakfast Bowl

Ingredients

2 eggs (lightly beaten)

1 onion (sliced)

½ teaspoon smoked paprika

1 avocado (diced)

10 black olives (pitted, diced)

6 mushrooms (sliced)

5 ¼ oz ground beef

Salt and pepper to taste

Coconut oil for cooking

Instructions:

- Heat oil in a skillet and sauté the onions and mushrooms in it with some salt and pepper for 2 minutes.

- Add the beef and paprika, and cook till the beef is no longer pink. Transfer to a platter.

- Pour the eggs into the skillet, scrambling it until desired doneness and then return the beef mixture back to the skillet.

- Mix in the olives and avocados, cooking for a minute.

Makes: 1 serving

Nutritional information per serving:

Calories: 616; Total Fat: 37.9 g; Carbohydrates: 25.9 g; Proteins: 51.5 g

Pineapple & Orange Smoothie

Ingredients

1 orange (peeled)

2/3 cups fresh pineapple (cubed)

2 celery stalks (chopped)

1 cup raw kale

8 oz water (filtered)

Instructions:

- Combine all the ingredients in a high speed blender and blend until smooth.

Makes: 1 serving

Nutritional information per serving:

Calories: 143.8; Total Fat: 0.63 g; Carbohydrates: 35.6 g; Proteins: 3.1 g

Apple & Chicken Omelette

Ingredients

1 teaspoon coconut oil

8 egg whites

5 ¼ oz cooked chicken breast (shredded)

1 apple (cored, peeled, diced)

3 collard leaves (stems discarded, finely chopped)

¾ oz hazelnuts (toasted, crushed)

Salt and pepper to taste

Instructions:

- Heat coconut oil in a skillet and sauté the chicken in it until golden brown.

- Mix in the apple and cook for ½ minute. Transfer onto a platter.

- Add the collards to the skillet and cook for ½ minute.

- Return the chicken mixture back to the skillet and pour the egg whites over.

- Sprinkle the hazelnuts, reduce the flame and cook covered loosely for around 5 minutes.

Makes: 1 serving

Nutritional information per serving:

Calories: 587; Total Fat: 23.5 g; Carbohydrates: 33.3 g; Proteins: 62.6 g

CHAPTER 2

Whole Food Lunch Recipes

Squash & Carrot Soup

Ingredients

1 onion (chopped)

4 cups vegetable broth

3 carrots (peeled, chopped)

3 garlic cloves (minced)

1 butternut squash (peeled, seeded, chopped)

Instructions:

- Combine all the ingredients in a slow cooker.

- Cook for 6-8 hours on low.

- Blend in batches using an immersion blender.

Makes: 6 servings

Nutritional information per serving:

Calories: 62; Total Fat: 0 g; Carbohydrates: 15 g; Proteins: 2 g

Chicken Chili

Ingredients

2 ½ lbs chicken breast (boneless, skinless)

1 onion (minced)

4 garlic cloves (minced)

2 jalapeno (diced)

2 poblano peppers (diced)

½ cup cilantro (chopped)

2 teaspoon cumin

1 teaspoon oregano

1 lime

6 cups chicken broth (low-sodium)

Salt and pepper to taste

Instructions:

- Combine all the ingredients in a slow cooker.

- Cook for 4 hours on low.

- Shred the chicken and return it back to the cooker.

Makes: 6 servings

Nutritional information per serving:

Calories: 258; Total Fat: 3 g; Carbohydrates: 11 g; Proteins: 46 g

Tomato & Red Pepper Soup

Ingredients

2 carrots (peeled, chopped)

2 celery stalks (chopped)

1 onion (chopped)

4 garlic cloves (minced)

72 oz can whole tomatoes (along with juices)

14 oz roasted red peppers (in water)

¼ cup basil (fresh)

4 cups vegetable broth

Salt and pepper to taste

1 bay leaf

Instructions:

- Combine all the ingredients in a slow cooker.

- Cook for 8 hours on low.

- Using an immersion blender, blend the soup in batches.

Makes: 8 servings

Nutritional information per serving:

Calories: 75; Total Fat: 1 g; Carbohydrates: 17 g; Proteins: 3 g

Grilled Spicy Broccoli

Ingredients

4 cups broccoli florets

½ tablespoon garlic powder

½ tablespoon kosher salt

½ tablespoon black pepper

¼ teaspoon red pepper flakes

2 tablespoon olive oil

Instructions:

- Toss together all the ingredients and spread it in a greased baking pan.

- Grill for 8-10 minutes until crispy tender.

Makes: 4 servings

Nutritional information per serving:

Calories: 96; Total Fat: 7 g; Carbohydrates: 7 g; Proteins: 3 g

Beef Chili

Ingredients

2 lbs ground beef (95% lean)

2 cups beef broth

1 ½ cups water

½ tablespoon olive oil

½ onion (minced)

2 garlic cloves (minced)

1 green pepper (chopped)

1 poblano pepper (seeded, chopped)

½ teaspoon cumin

2 teaspoon chilli powder

½ teaspoon salt

½ cup salsa

14 oz roasted diced tomatoes (canned)

2 zucchini (chopped)

Instructions:

- Heat the oil in a pot and sauté the garlic, onion and poblano pepper in it for 2-3 minutes.

- Mix in the beef and stir cook until browned.

- Mix in the rest of the ingredients and leave to simmer for around 20 minutes.

Makes: 6 servings

Nutritional information per serving:

Calories: 275; Total Fat: 9 g; Carbohydrates: 12 g; Proteins: 37 g

Tomato & Chicken Lettuce Wraps

Ingredients

2 ½ lbs chicken breast (boneless, skinless)

1 onion (minced)

20 oz fire roasted crushed tomatoes

3 tablespoon chipotle peppers in adobo sauce

1 teaspoon oregano

1 teaspoon garlic powder

½ teaspoon coriander

½ teaspoon cumin

Salt and pepper to taste

Instructions:

- Season the chicken with salt and pepper.

- Add the chicken to a crock pot with the rest of the ingredients.

- Cook on low for 4 hours.

- Shred the chicken and return to the crock pot, mixing well.

- Divide mixture into lettuce leaves and serve.

Makes: 6 servings

Nutritional information per serving:

Calories: 216; Total Fat: 2 g; Carbohydrates: 10 g; Proteins: 41 g

Root Veggies

Ingredients

1 lb sweet potatoes (chopped)

1 lb parsnips (chopped)

1 lb carrots (chopped)

1 rutabaga (peeled, chopped)

1 onion (chopped)

4 garlic cloves (minced)

¼ cup apple juice (unsweetened)

¼ cup balsamic vinegar

¼ cup water

Salt and pepper to taste

1 tablespoon olive oil

Instructions:

- Combine all the ingredients in a slow cooker.

- Cook for 6-8 hours on low.

Makes: 6 servings

Nutritional information per serving:

Calories: 221; Total Fat: 3 g; Carbohydrates: 47 g; Proteins: 4 g

Lemon Chicken & Artichoke Soup

Ingredients

1 lb chicken breast (skinless, boneless)

1 lb chicken thighs (skinless, boneless)

14 oz canned artichoke hearts (packed in water, drained)

1 onion (diced)

2 carrots (diced)

2 celery ribs (diced)

3 garlic cloves (minced)

1 bay leaf

½ teaspoon salt

½ teaspoon pepper

3 cups turnips (peeled, cubed)

6 cups chicken broth (low-sodium)

¼ cup freshly squeezed lemon juice

¼ cup parsley (chopped)

Instructions:

- Combine all the ingredients in a slow cooker leaving aside the parsley and lemon juice.

- Cook for 8 hours on low.

- Remove, shred the chicken and return back to the cooker.

- Mix in the parsley and lemon juice.

Makes: 6 servings

Nutritional information per serving:

Calories: 285; Total Fat: 5 g; Carbohydrates: 14 g; Proteins: 37 g

Parsley Veggie Salad

Ingredients

1 tablespoon olive oil

1 lemon (juiced)

½ cup parsley (chopped)

¼ cup red onion (sliced)

2 Roma tomatoes

4 Persian cucumbers (chopped)

1 tablespoon zaatar spice blend

Salt and pepper to taste

Instructions:

- Combine all the ingredients in a bowl and toss together.

Makes: 4 servings

Nutritional information per serving:

Calories: 71; Total Fat: 4 g; Carbohydrates: 8 g; Proteins: 1 g

Tomato & Avocado Salad

Ingredients

1 lb cherry tomatoes (halved)

1 cup avocado

1 English cucumber (chopped)

1 lime (juiced)

1 tablespoon lime juice

1 teaspoon salt

1 teaspoon cumin

½ teaspoon pepper

Instructions:

- Combine all the ingredients in a bowl and toss together.

Makes: 4 servings

Nutritional information per serving:

Calories: 97; Total Fat: 6 g; Carbohydrates: 12 g; Proteins: 3 g

Thai Sausage Soup

Ingredients

1 butternut squash (cubed)	4 cups vegetable broth
1 onion (diced)	6 lean chicken sausages (sliced, browned)
2 garlic cloves (sliced)	8 oz fresh spinach (chopped)
14 oz lite canned coconut milk	3 tablespoon red curry paste

Instructions:

- Combine the onion, garlic, squash, salt, pepper and vegetable broth in a slow cooker.

- Cook for 8 hours on low.

- Puree the soup using an immersion blender and then mix in the curry paste and coconut milk.

- Mix in the spinach and sausage and cook for 30 minutes.

Makes: 6 servings

Nutritional information per serving:

Calories: 253; Total Fat: 10 g; Carbohydrates: 20 g; Proteins: 17 g

Mushroom & Chicken Soup

Ingredients

2 lbs chicken thighs (boneless, skinless)

32 oz chicken broth (low-sodium)

14 oz fire roasted diced tomatoes (canned)

2 red peppers (diced)

2 green peppers (diced)

1 onion (thinly sliced)

2 cups mushrooms (sliced)

3 garlic cloves (minced)

1 jalapeno (seeded, minced)

2 teaspoon cumin

1 ½ teaspoon chilli powder

1 teaspoon paprika

1 teaspoon oregano

½ teaspoon coriander

Salt and pepper to taste

Instructions:

- Combine all the ingredients in a slow cooker.

- Cook for 6 hours on low.

- Shred the chicken and add it back to the soup.

Makes: 6 servings

Nutritional information per serving:

Calories: 265; Total Fat: 7 g; Carbohydrates: 14 g; Proteins: 34 g

Fruit & Nut Chicken Salad Recipe

Ingredients

1 ½ lb skinless, boneless cooked chicken breast (shredded)

2 cups seedless red grapes (halved)

¼ cup red onion (chopped)

¼ cup mayonnaise (Whole Food compliant)

½ cup walnuts (roasted)

1 avocado (diced)

2 teaspoon lemon juice

Salt and pepper to taste

Instructions:

- Toss together all the ingredients in a bowl.

Makes: 6 servings

Nutritional information per serving:

Calories: 431; Total Fat: 25 g; Carbohydrates: 13 g; Proteins: 36 g

Cumin Cauliflower Soup

Ingredients

1 tablespoon olive oil

4 garlic cloves (minced)

1 onion (diced)

1 tablespoon ginger (minced)

1 ½ teaspoon cumin

¼ teaspoon coriander

½ teaspoon

4 cups vegetable broth

2 lbs cauliflower florets

¼ cup cilantro

1 cup light canned coconut milk

Black pepper to taste

Instructions:

- Heat oil in a pot and sauté the onions in it for 4 minutes.

- Add the ginger, garlic, coriander, cumin and salt and cook for 2 minutes.

- Mix in the cauliflower and broth, cooking for another 10-15 minutes.

- Blend the soup until smooth using an immersion blender.

- Mix in the coconut milk and cilantro.

- Season with some pepper.

Makes: 6 servings

Nutritional information per serving:

Calories: 105; Total Fat: 6 g; Carbohydrates: 13 g; Proteins: 3 g

Salmon & Avocado Salad

Ingredients

1 lb boneless, skinless salmon

Salt and pepper to taste

1 lemon

1 tablespoon olive oil

2 tablespoon balsamic vinegar

6 cups kale

1 apple (chopped)

1 tomato (chopped)

1 cucumber (chopped)

¼ cup green onions (chopped)

1 sweet potato

½ avocado

Instructions:

- Squeeze some lemon juice over the salmon and season it with salt and pepper.

- Cook below the preheated broiler for 6-8 minutes till flaky.

- Combine the olive oil, balsamic vinegar and the rest of the lemon juice and massage it into the kale for 2 minutes.

- Using the fork, pierce the sweet potato and then microwave it for 4 minutes till tender. Chop.

- Toss together all the ingredients in a bowl.

Makes: 4 servings

Nutritional information per serving:

Calories: 387; Total Fat: 15 g; Carbohydrates: 37 g; Proteins: 30 g

Turkey Lettuce Wraps

Ingredients

½ cup onion (minced)

2 garlic cloves (minced)

1 green pepper (diced)

1.33 lbs ground turkey (93% lean)

1 teaspoon cumin

1 teaspoon salt

1 teaspoon chilli powder

1 teaspoon paprika

½ teaspoon oregano

½ teaspoon garlic powder

½ teaspoon onion powder

¼ teaspoon coriander

½ cup chicken broth

½ cup tomato sauce (canned)

1 romaine lettuce head

2 tomatoes (diced)

¼ cup cilantro

Instructions:

- Heat a skillet and sauté the garlic, onions, turkey and pepper until the turkey is no longer pink.

- Add the broth, spices and tomato sauce, bringing it to a simmer.

- Cook until the sauce thickens for around 8-10 minutes.

- Divide the cooked mixture among lettuce leaves, topping it with cilantro and tomatoes.

Makes: 4 servings

Nutritional information per serving:

Calories: 272; Total Fat: 13 g; Carbohydrates: 9 g; Proteins: 30 g

Sausage & Spinach Soup

Ingredients

2 teaspoon olive oil

1 lb lean turkey sausage

1 onion (diced)

2 carrots (chopped)

2 celery stalks (chopped)

1 red pepper (chopped)

1 green pepper (chopped)

3 garlic cloves (minced)

14 oz diced Italian tomatoes (canned, undrained)

2 cups low-sodium chicken broth

½ teaspoon oregano

1 bay leaf

4 cups spinach

Salt and pepper to taste

Instructions:

- Heat oil in a pot and sauté the sausage in it for 5-6 minutes until browned.

- Add the carrots, onion, garlic and celery, cooking for 5-6 minutes.

- Add the broth, oregano, bay leaf and tomatoes with juice and bring to simmer.

- Leave to simmer covered for 20 minutes.

- Mix in the spinach, stirring until wilted.

- Season with salt and pepper.

Makes: 4 servings

Nutritional information per serving:

Calories: 291; Total Fat: 12 g; Carbohydrates: 18 g; Proteins: 27 g

Spinach & Berry Salad

Ingredients

3 cups spinach

2 chicken breasts (grilled, diced)

2/3 cups blueberries

2/3 cups strawberries

2/3 cups raspberries

1 avocado (diced)

1 shallot (sliced)

¼ cup slivered almonds

Salt and pepper to taste

Dressing:

1/3 cup blueberries

¼ cup olive oil

3 tablespoon lime juice

1/8 cup apple cider vinegar

Instructions:

- For the dressing first process the blueberries in the processor and then add the rest of the dressing ingredients processing until smooth.

- Combine all the salad ingredients in a bowl and toss together.

- Pour the dressing over and toss again.

Makes: 2 servings

Nutritional information per serving:

Calories: 710; Total Fat: 54 g; Carbohydrates: 28 g; Proteins: 34 g

Cucumber & Tomato Salad

Ingredients

2 cucumbers (peeled, sliced thinly)

2 cup grape tomatoes (halved)

½ red onion (sliced thinly)

Sea salt to taste

¼ teaspoon black pepper

2 tablespoons fresh dill

2 tablespoons white balsamic vinegar

1 tablespoon extra-virgin olive oil

1 teaspoon mustard (with no added sugar)

Instructions:

- Toss together the tomatoes, cucumber and onion in a bowl.

- In another bowl, whisk together the rest of the ingredients to make the dressing.

- Pour the dressing over the salad and toss again.

Makes: 5 servings

Nutritional information per serving:

Calories: 66; Total Fat: 4 g; Carbohydrates: 7 g; Proteins: 1 g

Shrimps Stuffed in Avocado

Ingredients

28 shrimps (cleaned & deveined)

½ red onion (sliced)

2 garlic cloves (crushed)

12 grape tomatoes (halved)

2 tablespoon cilantro (finely chopped)

1 teaspoon kosher salt

1 tablespoon olive oil

¼ cup white wine vinegar

½ jalapeno (finely diced)

2 tablespoon clam juice

1/8 teaspoon cumin

1/8 teaspoon pepper

4 cups arugula

2 avocados

Instructions:

- Cook the shrimps in a pot of water for around 4 minutes and then transfer to ice bath.
- Combine the garlic, onions, cilantro, tomatoes, salt, vinegar, jalapeno, olive oil, cumin, pepper and clam juice in a bowl.
- Mix in the shrimps and then refrigerate overnight.
- Chop the avocados into half, discarding the skin and pit.
- Spread arugula on 4 serving plates, place ½ avocado over it and then top each avocado half with the shrimp mixture.

Makes: 4 servings

Nutritional information per serving:

Calories: 254; Total Fat: 16 g; Carbohydrates: 13 g; Proteins: 18 g

Cucumber & Strawberry Salad

Ingredients

¼ cup red onion (slivered)

1 1/3 cup strawberries (sliced)

1 1/3 cup cucumber (diced)

1 teaspoon fresh mint (chopped)

1 teaspoon fresh lime juice

Pinch of kosher salt

Freshly ground black pepper to taste

1 tablespoon balsamic glaze

2 tablespoon sliced almonds (toasted)

Instructions:

- Toss together all the ingredients in a salad bowl.

Makes: 4 servings

Nutritional information per serving:

Calories: 47; Total Fat: 1.5 g; Carbohydrates: 7 g; Proteins: 1 g

Avocado & Shrimp Salad

Ingredients

¼ cup red onion (chopped)

2 limes (juiced)

1 teaspoon olive oil

1 lb jumbo shrimps (peeled, cooked, chopped)

1 tomato (diced)

1 avocado (diced)

1 jalapeno (seeds discarded, diced)

1 tablespoon cilantro (chopped)

¼ teaspoon kosher salt

Freshly ground black pepper to taste

Instructions:

- Mix together the lime juice, salt, pepper, olive oil and red onion in a bowl, leaving to marinate for 5 minutes.

- Toss together the rest of the ingredients in a salad bowl.

- Pour the marinated mixture over and toss again.

Makes: 4 servings

Nutritional information per serving:

Calories: 197; Total Fat: 8 g; Carbohydrates: 7 g; Proteins: 25 g

Spicy Chicken in Lettuce Wraps

Ingredients

¼ cup hot cayenne pepper sauce

6 Iceberg lettuce leaves

1 ½ cups carrot (shredded)

2 celery stalks (thinly sliced)

Chicken:

24 oz chicken breast (skinless, boneless)

1 celery stalk

½ onion (diced)

1 garlic clove

16 oz fat-free chicken broth (low sodium)

Instructions:

- Combine all the chicken ingredients in a slow cooker and cook covered for 4 hours on high.

- Retain only half cup broth in the cooker. Shred the chicken and return to the cooker along with the cayenne sauce.

- Cook for 30 minutes on high.

- Distribute the chicken between the lettuce leaves and top it with the celery and carrots.

Makes: 6 servings

Nutritional information per serving:

Calories: 147.7; Total Fat: 0.1 g; Carbohydrates: 5.2 g; Proteins: 24.9 g

Asparagus & Lobster Salad

Ingredients

8 oz lobster (cooked, chopped)

3 ½ cups asparagus (chopped, steamed)

2 tablespoon lemon juice

4 teaspoons extra-virgin olive oil

¼ teaspoon kosher salt

Black pepper to taste

½ cup cherry tomatoes (halved)

1 basil leaf (chopped)

2 tablespoon red onion (diced)

Instructions:

- Whisk together the lemon juice, salt, pepper and oil in a bowl.

- Toss together the rest of the ingredients in a salad bowl.

- Pour the dressing over and toss again.

Makes: 2 servings

Nutritional information per serving:

Calories: 247; Total Fat: 10.5 g; Carbohydrates: 14 g; Proteins: 27 g

Whole Food Approved Bacon & Avocado Sprout Salad

Ingredients

3 cups Brussels sprouts (shredded)

4 oz avocado (diced)

3 slices Whole Food Approved bacon (no sugar added; diced, cooked until crispy)

Dressing:

4 teaspoons olive oil

½ teaspoon kosher salt

2 tablespoon red onion (chopped)

1 teaspoon mustard (no added sugar)

2 tablespoon + 1 teaspoon red wine vinegar

Instructions:

- Whisk together all the dressing ingredients in a bowl.

- Toss together the rest of the ingredients in a salad bowl.

- Pour the dressing over and toss again.

Makes: 2 servings

Nutritional information per serving:

Calories: 284; Total Fat: 21 g; Carbohydrates: 18.5 g; Proteins: 10 g

Creamy Squash Soup

Ingredients

16 oz kobacha squash (halved, seeds discarded)

16 oz butternut squash (halved, seeds discarded)

2 shallots (quartered)

2 cups chicken broth

¾ cup light coconut milk

Pinch of nutmeg

Instructions:

- Combine the broth, shallots and squash in a slow cooker and cook for 4 hours on high.

- Discard the skin of the squash.

- Mix in the rest of the ingredients.

- Using an immersion blender, blend the soup until smooth and creamy.

Makes: 4 servings

Nutritional information per serving:

Calories: 152; Total Fat: 3 g; Carbohydrates: 35 g; Proteins: 3 g

Simple Garlicky- Cauliflower Soup

Ingredients

2 tablespoon olive oil

2 carrots (peeled, diced)

2 celery stalks (diced)

1 onion (diced)

1 cauliflower head (chopped)

2 bay leaves

4 cups chicken broth

1 cup almond milk

½ teaspoon cumin

½ teaspoon fresh thyme

1 teaspoon oregano

Salt and pepper to taste

½ lb Whole Food Approved bacon (no sugar added; diced)

Instructions:

- Heat oil in a pot and sauté the onion, garlic, carrots and celery in it for 3-4 minutes, seasoning it with salt and pepper.

- Mix in the bay leaves and cauliflower and cook for another 3-4 minutes.

- Mix in the broth and almond milk, cooking for another few minutes.

- Bring to boil, reduce the flame and simmer for 12 minutes.

- Discard the bay leaves and puree the soup using an immersion blender.

- Mix in the rest of the ingredients.

Makes: 6 servings

Nutritional information per serving:

Calories: 404; Total Fat: 31.1 g; Carbohydrates: 12.9 g; Proteins: 19.6 g

Quick Tomato Salad

Ingredients

4 tomatoes (diced)

¼ red onion (diced)

2 garlic cloves (minced)

4 tablespoon extra-virgin olive oil

2 tablespoon fresh parsley (chopped)

Salt to taste

Instructions:

- Toss together all the ingredients in a salad bowl.

Makes: 4 servings

Nutritional information per serving:

Calories: 74; Total Fat: 7.1 g; Carbohydrates: 3.1 g; Proteins: 0.6 g

Leek & Potato Soup

Ingredients

1 tablespoon olive oil

2 leeks (sliced thinly)

2 garlic cloves (minced)

3 potatoes (peeled, cubed)

2 cups vegetable broth

2 cups almond milk

Salt and pepper to taste

4 Whole Food Approved bacon strips (no sugar added; cooked, crumbled)

Instructions:

- Heat the oil in a soup pot and sauté the leeks in it for around 5 minutes, seasoning it with salt and pepper.

- Add the garlic, potatoes, broth and bring to boil.

- Simmer covered for 10 minutes and then add the almond milk.

- Puree the soup using an immersion blender.

- Serve garnished with the bacon.

Makes: 8 servings

Nutritional information per serving:

Calories: 327; Total Fat: 21.2 g; Carbohydrates: 19.5 g; Proteins: 16.8 g

Tomato & Cantaloupe Gazpacho

Ingredients

3 tomatoes (quartered)

½ cantaloupe (peeled, diced)

2 seedless cucumbers (chopped)

1 jalapeno pepper (seeds discarded)

1 garlic clove

1 tablespoon red wine vinegar

1 tablespoon olive oil

1 teaspoon salt

½ teaspoon ground black pepper

Handful of fresh basil leaves

Handful of fresh mint leaves

1 lime (juiced)

Instructions:

- Combine all the ingredients in a food processor.

- Process until smooth.

- Refrigerate overnight.

Makes: 4 servings

Nutritional information per serving:

Calories: 114; Total Fat: 4.1 g; Carbohydrates: 19.6 g; Proteins: 2.9 g

CHAPTER 3

Whole Food Dinner Recipes

Spinach Beef Balls

Ingredients

1 lb ground beef (99% lean)

10 oz frozen chopped spinach (defrosted, moisture squeezed out)

½ cup onion (minced)

4 garlic cloves (minced)

½ teaspoon salt

1 egg

½ teaspoon dried basil

¼ teaspoon oregano

¼ teaspoon pepper

Instructions:

- Combine all the ingredients in a bowl and mix well.

- Shape portions of the mixture into meat balls and place on a greased baking sheet.

- Bake in an oven preheated to 375 degrees Fahrenheit for 19-20 minutes.

Makes: 4 servings

Nutritional information per serving:

Calories: 198; Total Fat: 8 g; Carbohydrates: 5 g; Proteins: 29 g

Broccoli & Shrimps Stir Fry

Ingredients

4 teaspoon olive oil

2 lbs raw shrimps

3 teaspoon lemon pepper spice

¼ cup lemon juice

4 cups broccoli florets

2 tablespoon parsley (chopped)

Salt and pepper to taste

Instructions:

- Heat olive oil in a skillet and cook the shrimps in it for a minute.

- Add the lemon pepper spice and the lemon juice and cook for 3-4 minutes, stirring occasionally until the shrimps are cooked. Remove and place aside.

- Add the broccoli to the skillet and cook covered for another 3-4 minutes.

- Mix the shrimps back in and toss.

- Mix in the parsley and season with salt and pepper.

Makes: 4 servings

Nutritional information per serving:

Calories: 319; Total Fat: 9 g; Carbohydrates: 9 g; Proteins: 49 g

Crispy Pork Crusted with Almond

Ingredients

1.33 lbs lean pork chops (boneless)

3 tablespoon Dijon mustard

2 egg whites (whisked)

1/3 cup almond meal

½ teaspoon salt

½ teaspoon pepper

2 teaspoon olive oil

¾ teaspoon dried thyme

Instructions:

- Mix the salt, pepper, thyme and mustard.

- Coat the pork with the mustard mixture.

- Dip the pork chops first into the egg and then dredge it in the almond meal.

- Heat olive oil in a skillet and lightly fry the pork chops in it until crispy brown for 2-3 minutes per side.

- Transfer the skillet into an oven preheated to 450 degrees Fahrenheit for 9-10 minutes.

Makes: 4 servings

Nutritional information per serving:

Calories: 287; Total Fat: 14 g; Carbohydrates: 2 g; Proteins: 38 g

Pork Chops & Peach Salsa

Ingredients

1.33 lbs lean center-cut pork chops (boneless)

2 tablespoon olive oil

1 teaspoon chilli powder

½ teaspoon salt

½ teaspoon pepper

Salsa:

2 peaches (chopped)

¼ red onion (chopped)

2 tablespoon cilantro

1 tablespoon lime juice

Instructions:

- Brush the pork with olive oil and season it with salt, pepper and chilli powder.

- Grill on a preheated grill for 4-5 minutes per side.

- For the salsa, toss together all the salsa ingredients in a bowl.

- Serve the pork topped with the salsa.

Makes: 4 servings

Nutritional information per serving:

Calories: 287; Total Fat: 12 g; Carbohydrates: 9 g; Proteins: 35 g

Chicken Braised in Tomato

Ingredients

1.33 lbs chicken thighs (boneless, skinless)

2 teaspoon olive oil

½ cup onion (sliced)

1 green pepper (sliced)

6 garlic cloves (chopped)

20 oz canned crushed tomatoes

1 cup chicken broth (low-sodium)

2 thyme sprigs

Salt and pepper to taste

Instructions:

- Season the chicken with salt and pepper.

- Heat a non-stick skillet and cook the chicken in it for 3-4 minutes per side. Transfer to a platter.

- Heat the olive oil and sauté the garlic, onion and green pepper in it for 2 minutes.

- Mix in the thyme, tomatoes and chicken broth, bringing to a simmer.

- Place the chicken pieces in the sauce.

- Cook covered for 30 minutes on low flame until the chicken is completely cooked.

Makes: 4 servings

Nutritional information per serving:

Calories: 276; Total Fat: 9 g; Carbohydrates: 16 g; Proteins: 33 g

Mushroom Tilapia Burgers

Ingredients

1 lb tilapia	½ teaspoon black pepper
1 egg	1 teaspoon paprika
1 egg white	½ teaspoon basil
2 tablespoon flaxseed meal	1 teaspoon onion powder
2 tablespoon Dijon mustard	1 teaspoon vegetable oil
2 garlic cloves (minced)	1 avocado (chopped)
1 teaspoon salt	8 portabella mushrooms

Instructions:

- Grease the mushrooms with cooking spray and season it with some salt and pepper.

- Cook the mushrooms until tender for 10-12 minutes.

- Place the fish in a food processor and process until chopped.

- Mix fish, egg, egg white, flaxseed meal, salt, pepper, garlic, mustard, basil, paprika and onion powder in a bowl.

- Shape portions of the mixture into patties and brush it with vegetable oil.

- Cook the tilapia burgers in a skillet for around 4-5 minutes per side.

- Serve the burgers over the mushrooms.

- Top with the avocado.

Makes: 2 servings

Nutritional information per serving:

Calories: 276; Total Fat: 13 g; Carbohydrates: 13 g; Proteins: 29 g

Spiced Salmon

Ingredients

30 oz coho salmon fillets (skinless)

¼ teaspoon salt

¼ teaspoon pepper

¼ teaspoon smoked paprika

¼ teaspoon ground ginger

¾ teaspoon ground cumin

2 ½ teaspoon olive oil

2 ½ teaspoon chilli powder

Instructions:

- Mix all the dry spices in a bowl.

- Spray the salmon with cooking spray and rub the spice mixture into it.

- Heat oil in a pan and cook the salmon fillets in it for 4-5 minutes per side.

Makes: 5 servings

Nutritional information per serving:

Calories: 274; Total Fat: 12 g; Carbohydrates: 1 g; Proteins: 37 g

Salmon Crusted with Coconut

Ingredients

30 oz salmon (skinless, boneless)

1/3 cup unsweetened coconut (shredded)

2 egg whites (whisked)

Salt and pepper to taste

Instructions:

- Season the salmon with salt and pepper.

- Dip the salmon into the egg and then dredge it with the coconut.

- Arrange the fish on a wire rack placed over a baking dish.

- Bake for 10-12 minutes in an oven preheated to 400 degrees Fahrenheit.

Makes: 5 servings

Nutritional information per serving:

Calories: 293; Total Fat: 14 g; Carbohydrates: 1 g; Proteins: 39 g

Pork Cauliflower Rice

Ingredients

4 cups cauliflower florets (riced)

2 teaspoon vegetable oil

1 teaspoon sesame oil

1 tablespoon raw ginger (minced)

4 garlic cloves (minced)

1 ½ lb lean pork tenderloin (chopped into strips)

2 eggs

2 egg whites

5 green onions (chopped)

½ cup red onions (diced)

2 cups green cabbage (shredded)

¼ cup water

2 tablespoon coconut aminos

Instructions:

- Whisk together the eggs and egg whites, seasoning it with salt and pepper.

- Heat teaspoon of vegetable oil in a pan and cook the eggs until they are just scrambled. Transfer to a bowl.

- Cook the pork in the pan of 2-3 minutes per side and place aside.

- Add the rest of the vegetable oil and the sesame oil.

- Sauté the red onions, cauliflower, ginger, garlic, green onions and green cabbage in it.

- Add ¼ cup water and cook for 5 minutes.

- Mix in the pork, eggs and coconut aminos, cooking for another minute.

Makes: 4 servings

Nutritional information per serving:

Calories: 328; Total Fat: 10 g; Carbohydrates: 13 g; Proteins: 46 g

Chicken Fajita Bake

Ingredients

1.33 lbs chicken breasts (skinless, boneless, chopped into strips)

14 oz can diced tomatoes with green chilies

1 onion (sliced)

1 green pepper (sliced)

1 cup mushrooms

2 teaspoon olive oil

1 ½ teaspoon chilli powder

1 ½ teaspoon cumin

1 teaspoon paprika

½ teaspoon garlic powder

½ teaspoon onion powder

½ teaspoon dried oregano

¼ teaspoon salt

Instructions:

- Combine all the ingredients in a casserole dish and toss together using your hands.

- Bake in an oven preheated to 400 degrees Fahrenheit for around 25-30 minutes.

Makes: 4 servings

Nutritional information per serving:

Calories: 226; Total Fat: 4 g; Carbohydrates: 12 g; Proteins: 35 g

Spaghetti Squash, Zucchini & Turkey Curry

Ingredients

4 cups spaghetti squash

1 lb ground turkey (99% lean)

½ cup onion (minced)

2 cups zucchini (chopped)

4 cups fresh spianch

2 garlic cloves (minced)

3 tablespoon green curry paste

1 cup canned lite coconut milk

1 lime (juiced)

1 tablespoon fresh ginger (minced)

Instructions:

- Spray the squash with cooking spray and place on a baking sheet lined with foil.

- Bake in an oven preheated to 400 degrees Fahrenheit for 45-60 minutes.

- Scrape the squash using a fork.

- Heat a skillet and brown the turkey in it.

- Add the garlic, onion, seasoning with salt and pepper and cook for 3-4 minutes.

- Mix together the ginger, curry paste, coconut milk, lime juice and then add to the skillet along with the zucchini, cooking for 3-4 minutes.

- Mix in the spaghetti squash.

Makes: 4 servings

Nutritional information per serving:

Calories: 247; Total Fat: 7 g; Carbohydrates: 17 g; Proteins: 29 g

Beef Burgers

Ingredients

1 lb ground beef (95% lean)

1/3 cup onion (diced)

2 garlic cloves (minced)

½ teaspoon salt

½ teaspoon pepper

½ teaspoon oregano

¼ teaspoon red pepper flakes

1 egg

2 tablespoon fresh basil (chopped)

1 tablespoon tomato paste

1 teaspoon olive oil

Instructions:

- Whisk together the tomato paste and egg.

- Combine the rest of the ingredients except the oil in a bowl, mixing well.

- Add the egg mixture to the bowl and mix well.

- Shape portions of the mixture into patties and brush it with olive oil

- Grill the burgers in a non-stick skillet for 4-5 minutes per side.

Makes: 4 servings

Nutritional information per serving:

Calories: 179; Total Fat: 7 g; Carbohydrates: 3 g; Proteins: 26 g

Italian Pepperoncini Chicken

Ingredients

2.67 lbs chicken breast (skinless, boneless)

1 cup chicken broth (low-sodium)

2 tablespoon Italian seasoning

8 oz pepperoncinis with juice

Instructions:

- Combine all the ingredients in a slow cooker.

- Leave to cook for 4 hours on low.

- Slice and serve.

Makes: 8 servings

Nutritional information per serving:

Calories: 208; Total Fat: 2 g; Carbohydrates: 2 g; Proteins: 33 g

Chicken & Mushroom Delight

Ingredients

2 lbs chicken breast (skinless, boneless, chopped)

1 onion (thinly sliced)

2 celery stalks (diced)

4 tablespoon tomato paste

14 oz canned fire roasted tomatoes (diced)

1 lb mushrooms (sliced)

1 green pepper (chopped)

4 garlic cloves (sliced)

1 tablespoon Italian seasoning

½ cup red wine

1 ½ tablespoon capers (drained)

½ teaspoon red pepper flakes

1 cup black olives (Whole Food approved)

Instructions:

- Combine all the ingredients except the olives and chicken in a slow cooker.

- Season the chicken with salt and pepper and place in the cooker.

- Leave to cook for 4-6 hours on low.

- Add the olives, 30 minutes prior to the completion of cooking.

Makes: 6 servings

Nutritional information per serving:

Calories: 246; Total Fat: 4 g; Carbohydrates: 14 g; Proteins: 36 g

Citus Flavoured Chicken

Ingredients

4 lbs chicken legs (skin removed)

1/4 cup fresh lime juice

1/4 cup fresh orange juice

4 garlic cloves

2 tablespoon fresh thyme

1 tablespoon fresh ginger (minced)

1 teaspoon ground allspice

4 green onions

1 ½ teaspoon salt

2 tablespoon white vinegar

1 red pepper (seeded, chopped)

2 habanero peppers (chopped)

2 cups pineapple (chopped)

Instructions:

- Combine the lime juice, garlic, orange juice, allspice, ginger, thyme, onions, red pepper, habanero peppers and salt in a food processor, blending until blended well.

- Season the chicken with salt and pepper and place in the slow cooker along with the blended mixture.

- Leave to cook for 8 hours on low.

- Add the pineapple, 30 minutes prior to the completion of cooking.

Makes: 8 servings

Nutritional information per serving:

Calories: 321; Total Fat: 10 g; Carbohydrates: 11 g; Proteins: 44 g

Chicken Chili Verde

Ingredients

1 lb chicken breasts (skinless, boneless)

1 lb chicken thighs (skinless, boneless)

½ lb tomatillos (husked, quartered)

2 poblano peppers (seeded, chopped)

1 jalapeno pepper (seeded, chopped)

1 onion (sliced)

1/3 cup cilantro (chopped)

1 tablespoon coconut aminos

2 teaspoon cumin

Salt and Pepper, to taste

Instructions:

- Combine all the ingredients in a slow cooker.

- Leave to cook for 4 hours.

Makes: 6 servings

Nutritional information per serving:

Calories: 204; Total Fat: 4 g; Carbohydrates: 8 g; Proteins: 32 g

Beef Roast in White Vinegar

Ingredients

2 lbs top round beef roast (extra lean)

2 onions (sliced)

4 garlic cloves (sliced)

1 cup beef broth

2 tablespoon white vinegar

2 teaspoon dried oregano

1 teaspoon cumin

Salt and pepper to taste

Instructions:

- Season the beef with salt and pepper and place it in a slow cooker.

- Add the rest of the ingredients to the slow cooker.

- Leave to cook for 8 hours on low.

Makes: 6 servings

Nutritional information per serving:

Calories: 215; Total Fat: 5 g; Carbohydrates: 5 g; Proteins: 37 g

Sour & Spicy Beef

Ingredients

2 lbs top beef eye round (lean, trimmed of fat)

1 sweet onion (diced)

2 garlic cloves (sliced)

1 red bell pepper (diced)

2 jalapenos

¼ cup beef broth (low-sodium)

1 cup canned diced tomatoes with juice

1 tablespoon coconut aminos

2 tablespoon fresh lime juice

½ teaspoon cumin

¼ teaspoon oregano

¼ teaspoon coriander

Instructions:

- Season the beef with salt and pepper and place it in a slow cooker.

- Add the rest of the ingredients to the slow cooker.

- Leave to cook for 8 hours on low.

- Slice and serve.

Makes: 6 servings

Nutritional information per serving:

Calories: 233; Total Fat: 5 g; Carbohydrates: 8 g; Proteins: 36 g

Thai Style Ground Beef Curry

Ingredients

1 lb ground beef (95% lean)

1 leek (thinly sliced)

2 garlic cloves (minced)

1 teaspoon fresh ginger (raw)

1 tablespoon red curry paste

11/2 cups canned tomato sauce

1 teaspoon lime zest

1 tablespoon coconut aminos

½ cup canned light coconut milk

2 teaspoon lime juice

Instructions:

- Brown the beef in a skillet and then transfer it to a slow cooker.

- Add the rest of the ingredients to the slow cooker except the coconut milk and lime jucie.

- Leave to cook for 4 hours on low.

- Add the lime juice and coconut milk, stir and cook for another 15 minutes.

Makes: 4 servings

Nutritional information per serving:

Calories: 213; Total Fat: 8 g; Carbohydrates: 10 g; Proteins: 26 g

Spinach & Tomato Chicken

Ingredients

2 lbs chicken breast (boneless, skinless)

28 oz canned diced tomatoes, half juice drained

4 garlic cloves (minced)

1 sweet onion (thinly sliced)

3 tablespoon balsamic vinegar

1 tablespoon Italian seasoning

6 cups fresh spinach

Salt and pepper to taste

Instructions:

- Combine all the ingredients in a slow cooker except the spinach.

- Leave to cook for 4 hours on low.

- Add the spinach, 30 minutes prior to the completion of cooking.

Makes: 6 servings

Nutritional information per serving:

Calories: 227; Total Fat: 2 g; Carbohydrates: 12 g; Proteins: 35 g

Spinach & Tomato Turkey

Ingredients

1 ½ lbs ground turkey (99% lean)

3 garlic cloves (minced)

1 onion (diced)

2 carrots (diced)

1 teaspoon salt

3 jalapenos (whole)

1 lb potatoes (peeled, diced)

18 oz can tomato sauce

2 tablespoon chipotle peppers in adobo

1 bay leaf

1 black pepper ball

Instructions:

- Add the onion and turkey to a skillet and cook until the turkey is no longer pink.

- Add the garlic and stir cook for a minute.

- Transfer the mixture into a slow cooker.

- Combine the chipotle peppers and tomato sauce in a blender and blend. Add to the slow cooker.

- Add the rest of the ingredients to the slow cooker.

- Leave to cook for 4 hours on high.

Makes: 6 servings

Nutritional information per serving:

Calories: 228; Total Fat: 2 g; Carbohydrates: 23 g; Proteins: 30 g

Roasted Sweet Potatoes & Salmon

Ingredients

1.33 lbs raw wild salmon

2 tablespoon lemon juice

2 tablespoon Dijon mustard

1 teaspoon fresh dill

½ teaspoon oregano

1 tablespoon olive oil

1 lb sweet potatoes (thinly sliced)

1 lb asparagus

2 garlic cloves (minced)

Salt and pepper to taste

Instructions:

- Toss the potatoes and asparagus with salt, pepper and olive oil.

- Combine the mustard, lemon juice, oregano and dill in a bowl.

- Arrange the salmon in a baking pan and brush it with the mustard mix.

- Throw the veggies around the salmon.

- Bake in an oven preheated to 450 degrees Fahrenheit for 12-15 minutes.

Makes: 4 servings

Nutritional information per serving:

Calories: 382; Total Fat: 13 g; Carbohydrates: 28 g; Proteins: 37 g

Rosemary Flavoured Fingerling Potatoes

Ingredients

1.33 lbs fingerling potatoes

2 tablespoon olive oil

2 tablespoon fresh rosemary

¾ teaspoon kosher salt

½ teaspoon pepper

Instructions:

- Toss together all the ingredients and spread in a baking pan.

- Roast in an oven preheated to 450 degrees Fahrenheit for 45-60 minutes, shaking the pan often.

Makes: 4 servings

Nutritional information per serving:

Calories: 196; Total Fat: 7 g; Carbohydrates: 30 g; Proteins: 3 g

Grilled Zucchini

Ingredients

2 tablespoon olive oil

4 zucchini (chopped into pieces)

1 lemon (juice and zest)

2 teaspoon black pepper

1 teaspoon salt

1 teaspoon Italian seasoning

Instructions:

- Combine all the ingredients in a Ziploc bag and shake to coat the zucchini.

- Leave to marinate for 20 minutes.

- Place the zucchini directly on a preheated grill and cook for 3-5 minutes per side.

Makes: 4 servings

Nutritional information per serving:

Calories: 123; Total Fat: 8 g; Carbohydrates: 12 g; Proteins: 4 g

Paprika Mushroom Chicken

Ingredients

1 teaspoon olive oil

4 garlic cloves (minced)

2 carrots (peeled, chopped)

4 cups mushrooms (sliced)

2 red peppers (sliced)

2 tablespoon paprika

1.67 lbs chicken breast (skinless, boneless)

1 teaspoon salt

1 teaspoon pepper

1 cup chicken broth (non-fat)

¼ cup crushed almonds

Instructions:

- Heat oil a skillet and cook the carrots, garlic, mushrooms and red pepper in it for around 8 minutes.

- Add the paprika and stir cook for a minute.

- Season the chicken with salt and pepper and place in a crock pot.

- Add the mushroom mixture to the crock pot and pour the broth over.

- Leave to cook for 6 hours on low.

Makes: 5 servings

Nutritional information per serving:

Calories: 231; Total Fat: 4 g; Carbohydrates: 11 g; Proteins: 37 g

Shredded Pork & Cabbage

Ingredients

2 tablespoon olive oil

4 garlic cloves (whole)

2.67 lbs pork tenderloin (lean)

1 tablespoon salt

1 tablespoon liquid smoke

6 cups green cabbage (chopped)

½ cup water

Instructions:

- Rub the pork with salt, olive oil and liquid smoke.

- Add the water to the slow cooker and place the pork in it.

- Leave to cook for 8-10 hours on low, adding the cabbage prior to 2 hours of cooking completion.

- Shred the pork using a fork.

Makes: 8 servings

Nutritional information per serving:

Calories: 210; Total Fat: 7 g; Carbohydrates: 4 g; Proteins: 33 g

Baked Tilapia

Ingredients

2 tablespoon olive oil

1.33 lbs tilapia

2 tablespoon paprika

2 teaspoon onion powder

1 teaspoon black pepper

1 teaspoon chilli powder

½ teaspoon oregano

½ teaspoon dried thyme

½ teaspoon garlic powder

½ teaspoon salt

Instructions:

- Arrange the tilapia in a baking dish greased with cooking spray.

- Brush the oil onto the fish.

- Combine all the spices, mixing well and coat the fish on both sides with it.

- Bake in an oven preheated to 425 degrees Fahrenheit for 10-12 minutes.

Makes: 4 servings

Nutritional information per serving:

Calories: 193; Total Fat: 8 g; Carbohydrates: 4 g; Proteins: 29 g

Garlicky Mushrooms

Ingredients

1 tablespoon olive oil

1 lb mushrooms (quartered)

1 tablespoon ghee

2 garlic cloves (minced)

1 tablespoon balsamic vinegar

Salt and pepper to taste

Instructions:

- Combine the ghee and olive oil in a skillet and once melted add the mushrooms, stir cooking for 2-3 minutes until golden brown.

- Reduce the flame, add the rest of the ingredients and cook for another 2 minutes.

Makes: 4 servings

Nutritional information per serving:

Calories: 186; Total Fat: 7 g; Carbohydrates: 5 g; Proteins: 4 g

Roasted Sausage & Veggies

Ingredients

1 lb spicy sausage

2 medium sweet potatoes (peeled, chopped)

1 red bell pepper (chopped)

1 green bell pepper (chopped)

2 carrots (peeled, diced)

3 garlic cloves (minced)

3 tablespoon olive oil

1 teaspoon thyme

1 teaspoon basil

1 teaspoon red pepper flakes

Salt and pepper to taste

Instructions:

- Combine all the ingredients in a bowl and toss to coat.

- Spread the mixture on a baking sheet lined with foil.

- Bake in an oven preheated to 400 degrees Fahrenheit for 25 minutes, tossing the mixture halfway through.

Makes: 4 servings

Nutritional information per serving:

Calories: 606; Total Fat: 41.9 g; Carbohydrates: 33.6 g; Proteins: 23.9 g

Shrimp & Sausage Skillet

Ingredients

3 tablespoon olive oil

8 oz shrimps (peeled, deveined)

1 onion (diced)

1 red bell pepper (chopped)

1 green bell pepper (chopped)

1 zucchini (sliced)

10 oz spicy sausage

Salt and pepper to taste

2 tablespoon tomato paste

½ cup chicken broth

2 garlic cloves (minced)

½ teaspoon basil

½ teaspoon thyme

½ teaspoon oregano

¼ teaspoon red pepper flakes

Instructions:

- Heat a tablespoon of olive oil in a skillet and cook the shrimps in it for 5 minutes. Transfer to a platter.

- Add another tablespoon of oil and sauté the onions. Add the sausage and bell peppers and cook covered for 5 minutes, stirring often.

- Add the garlic and zucchini, stir mixing.

- Add the remaining ingredients and cook for 5-7 minutes.

- Mix in the shrimps and cook for an additional 3 minutes.

- Bake in an oven preheated to 400 degrees Fahrenheit for 25 minutes, tossing the mixture halfway through.

Makes: 4 servings

Nutritional information per serving:

Calories: 451; Total Fat: 31.4 g; Carbohydrates: 13.7g; Proteins: 29 g

Creamy Apple and Squash Soup

Serves: 4 Servings

Ingredients:

1 apple, chopped into chunks

1 small butternut squash, cut into halves and scoop

out seeds

1/4 cup coconut milk

5 cups vegetable stock

1/4 tsp garlic salt

1/4 tsp basil

1/4 tsp oregano

Pepper

Salt

Directions:

1. Preheat your oven at 200C.

2. Roast squash about 45 minutes or until tender.

3. While squash is roasting, add apple chunks in large pot with vegetable stock.

4. Bring to boil, and then simmer for 15 minutes or until apple are soft.

5. Scoop out roasted squash out of peel and place in blender along with apples and puree until smooth.

6. Pour back squash and apple puree into the pot and stir well.

7. Stir in spices, coconut milk and herbs.

8. Serve hot and enjoy.

Nutritional Value (Amount per Serving):

Calories 70, Fat 3.8 g, Carbohydrates 8.3 g, Sugar 5.1 g, Protein 1.0 g, Cholesterol 0 mg

Grilled Shrimp with Thyme in Foil

Serves: 6 Servings

Ingredients:

2 tbsp extra-virgin olive oil

2 pound shrimp, peeled

1 cup orange juice

1 tsp orange zest, grated

1 tbsp thyme, chopped

2 garlic cloves, minced

1 double layer aluminum foil, 18*24 in size

Pepper

Salt

Directions:

1. Spray foil with non-stick cooking spray.

2. Combine all ingredients in bowl and toss well set aside for 30 minutes.

3. Pour shrimp mixture in foil and fold the foil and seal completely.

4. Place packet on hot grill for 15 minutes.

5. Open packet carefully and serve.

Nutritional Value (Amount per Serving):

Calories 241, Fat 7.4 g, Carbohydrates 7.3 g, Sugar 3.5 g, Protein 34.8 g, Cholesterol 310 mg

30 Day Challenge Meal Plan

DAY	BREAKFAST	LUNCH	DINNER
1	_Sweet Potato & Sausage Breakfast Bake_ 25	_Lemon Chicken & Artichoke Soup_ 51	_Creamy Apple and Squash Soup_ 106
2	_Breakfast Bowl_ 13	_Beef Chili_ 48	_Thai Style Ground Beef Curry_ 94
3	_Berries & Nuts in Coconut Milk_ 18	_Cucumber & Strawberry Salad_ 64	_Grilled Zucchini_ 99
4	_Breakfast Chia Pudding_ 31	_Cucumber & Strawberry Salad_ 64	_Spiced Salmon_ 82
5	_Basil Zucchini Omelette_ 14	_Sausage & Spinach Soup_ 60	_Shredded Pork & Cabbage_ 101
6	_Spinach & Sweet Potato Breakfast Casserole_ 21	_Tomato & Red Pepper Soup_ 46	_Italian Pepperoncini Chicken_ 88
7	_Pineapple & Orange Smoothie_ 40	_Whole Food Approved Bacon & Avocado Sprout Salad_ 68	_Spaghetti Squash, Zucchini & Turkey Curry_ 86
8	_Carrot & Mixed Fruit Smoothie_ 12	_Fruit & Nut Chicken Salad Recipe_ 56	_Chicken Chili Verde_ 91
9	_Double-Baked Breakfast Potatoes_ 29	_Spicy Chicken in Lettuce Wraps_ 66	_Roasted Sweet Potatoes & Salmon_ 97
10	_Mexicana Breakfast Bowl_ 37	_Simple Garlicky-Cauliflower Soup_ 70	_Pork Chops & Peach Salsa_ 79

30 Day Challenge Meal Plan

DAY	BREAKFAST	LUNCH	DINNER
11	Sausage & Sweet Potato Scramble 16	Tomato & Avocado Salad 53	Spinach & Tomato Turkey 96
12	Pork & Blackberry Breakfast Sausage 27	Mushroom & Chicken Soup 55	Spinach Beef Balls 76
13	Butternut Sausage Breakfast Casserole 15	Spinach & Berry Salad 61	Roasted Sausage & Veggies 104
14	Breakfast Ham & Potato Frittata 33	Tomato & Cantaloupe Gazpacho 73	Chicken Braised in Tomato 80
15	Baked Mushroom Omelette 38	Turkey Lettuce Wraps 59	Crispy Pork Crusted with Almond 78
16	Breakfast Pork Sausages 30	Leek & Potato Soup 72	Spinach & Tomato Chicken 95
17	Apple & Chicken Omelette 41	Cucumber & Tomato Salad 62	Mushroom Tilapia Burgers 81
18	Breakfast Green Smoothie 23	Tomato & Chicken Lettuce Wraps 49	Broccoli & Shrimps Stir Fry 77
19	Whole Food Approved Bacon & Root Veggie Hash 28	Whole Food Approved Bacon & Avocado Sprout Salad 68	Garlicky Mushrooms 103
20	Egg & Beef Breakfast Bowl 39	Avocado & Shrimp Salad 65	Grilled Shrimp with Thyme in Foil 107

30 Day Challenge Meal Plan

DAY	BREAKFAST	LUNCH	DINNER
21	*Breakfast Veggie Frittata* 22	*Salmon & Avocado Salad* 58	*Beef Burgers* 87
22	*Sweet Potato & Chicken Sausage Hash* 24	*Squash & Carrot Soup* 44	*Salmon Crusted with Coconut* 83
23	*Almond Flavoured Banana & Coconut flakes* 17	*Root Veggies* 50	*Chicken Fajita Bake* 85
24	*Scotch Eggs* 36	*Asparagus & Lobster Salad* 67	*Rosemary Flavoured Fingerling Potatoes* 98
25	*Butter Sausage & Apple Hash* 20	*Grilled Spicy Broccoli* 47	*Pork Cauliflower Rice* 84
26	*Summer Veggie-Egg Breakfast* 34	*Chicken Chili* 45	*Chicken & Mushroom Delight* 89
27	*Vegetable & Avocado Scramble* 19	*Quick Tomato Salad* 71	*Sour & Spicy Beef* 93
28	*Chorizo & Kale Hash with Sweet Potatoes* 32	*Thai Sausage Soup* 54	*Citrus Flavoured Chicken* 90
29	*Coconut & Orange Omelette* 26	*Parsley Veggie Salad* 52	*Baked Tilapia* 102
30	*Asian Seafood Omelette* 35	*Creamy Squash Soup* 69	*Beef Roast in White Vinegar* 92

CPSIA information can be obtained
at www.ICGtesting.com
Printed in the USA
LVHW061752110720
660098LV00020B/268